PIANO . VOCAL . GUITAR

TOP DOWNLOADS 2010

ISBN 978-1-61780-769-5

HAL•LEONARD®
CORPORATION
7777 W. BLUEMOUND RD. P.O. BOX 13819 MILWAUKEE, WI 53213

Visit Hal Leonard Online at
www.halleonard.com

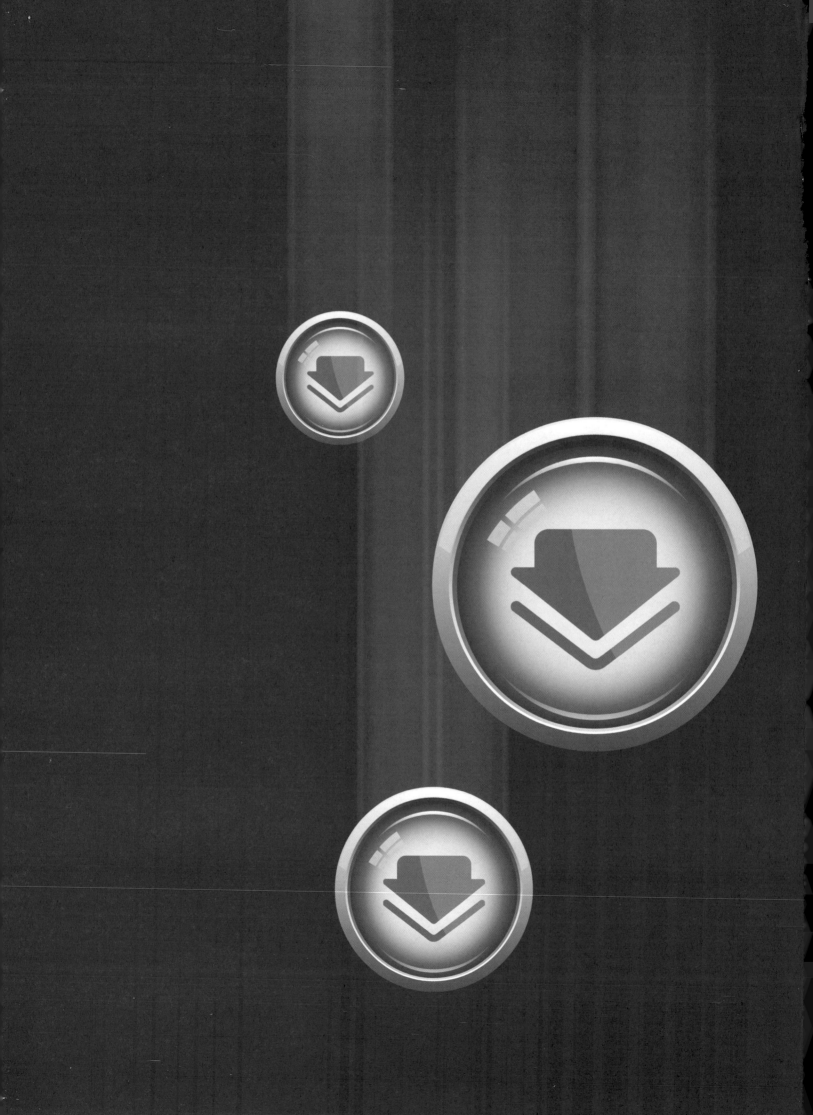

AIRPLANES

Words and Music by BOBBY RAY SIMMONS JR.,
ALEXANDER GRANT, JEREMY DUSSOLLIETY,
TIM SOMMERS and JUSTIN FRANKS

Additional Lyrics

Rap 1: Yeah, I could use a dream or a genie or a wish to go back to a place much simpler than this.
'Cause after all the partyin' and smashin' and crashin', and all the glitz and the glam and the fashion,
And all the pandemonium and all the madness, there comes a time where you fade to the blackness.
And when you starin' at that phone in your lap, and you hopin', but them people never call you back.
But that's just how the story unfolds, you get another hand soon after you fold.
And when your plans unravel in the sand, what would you wish for if you had one chance?
So, airplane, airplane, sorry I'm late. I'm on my way, so don't close that gate.
If I don't make that then I'll switch my flight and I'll be right back at it by the end of the night.
Chorus

Rap 2: Yeah, yeah, somebody take me back to the days before this was a job, before I got paid.
Before it ever mattered what I had in my bank, yeah, back when I was tryin' to get a tip at Subway.
And back when I was rappin' for the hell of it, but now-a-days we rappin' to stay relevant.
I'm guessin' that if we can make some wishes outta airplanes, then maybe, yo, maybe I'll go back to the days
Before the politics that we call the rap game, and back when ain't nobody listen to my mix tape,
And back before I tried to cover up my slang. But this is for Decatur, what's up Bobby Ray?
So can I get a wish to end the politics and get back to the music that started this sh*t?
So here I stand, and then again I say I'm hopin' we can make some wishes outta airplanes.
Chorus

BAD ROMANCE

Words and Music by STEFANI GERMANOTTA
and NADIR KHAYAT

Moderate Techno groove

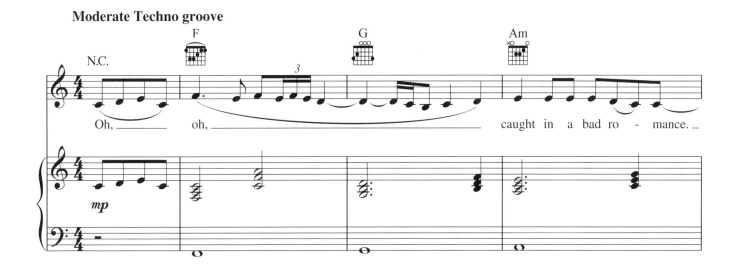

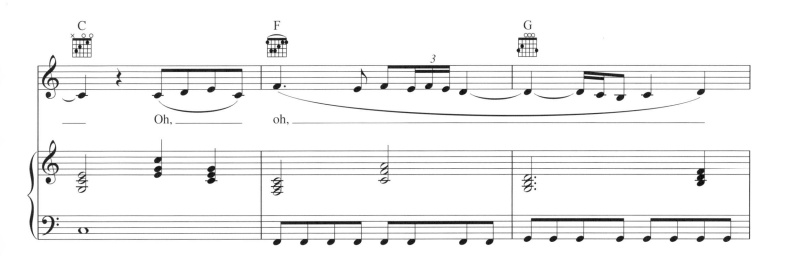

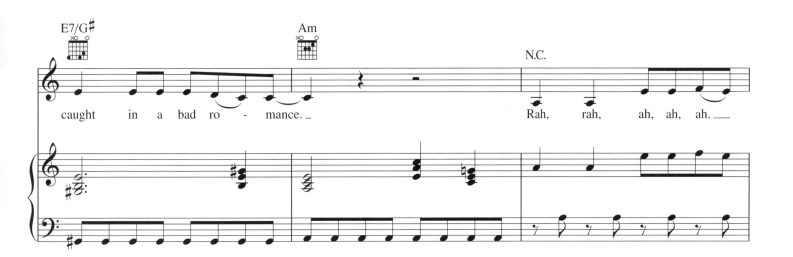

11

14

BREAK YOUR HEART

Words and Music by TAIO CRUZ,
CHRISTOPHER BRIDGES and FRASER T. SMITH

Additional Lyrics

Rap 1: Now I may not be the worst or the best but you gotta respect my honesty.
And I may break your heart but I don't really think there's anybody as bomb as me.
So you can take this chance. In the end everybody's gonna be wonderin' how you feel.
You might say this is Ludacris, but Taio Cruz, tell her how you feel.

Rap 2: That's all I'm gonna do woman.
Listen, now I'm only gonna break your heart and shatter and splatter it all into little bitty pieces.
Whether or not you get it all together, then it's finders keepers and losers weepers.
See, I'm not try'n' to lead you on. No, I'm only try'n' to keep it real.
You might say this is Ludacris, but Taio Cruz, tell her how you feel.

CALIFORNIA GURLS

Words and Music by MAX MARTIN,
LUKASZ GOTTWALD, BENJAMIN LEVIN,
CALVIN BROADUS and KATY PERRY

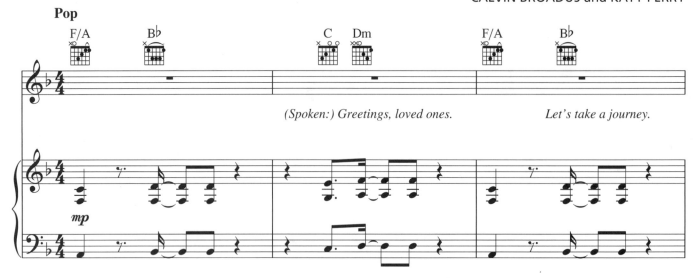

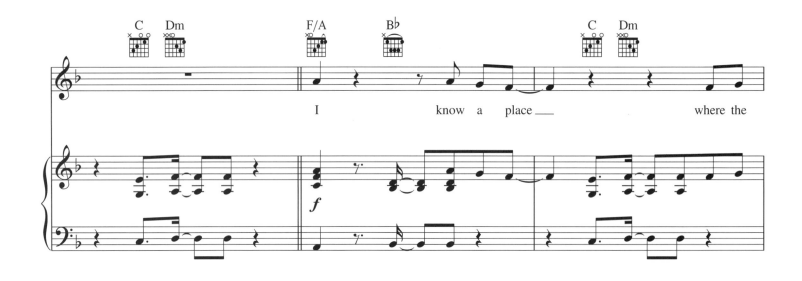

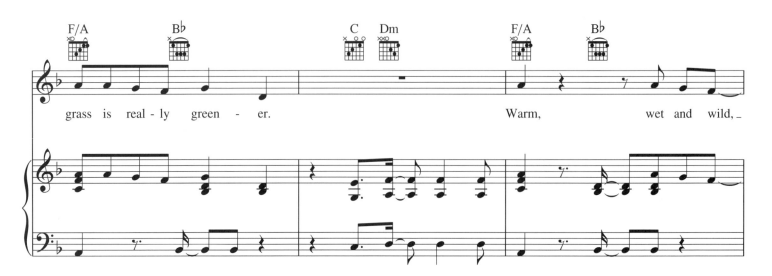

DYNAMITE

Words and Music by TAIO CRUZ,
LUKASZ GOTTWALD, MAX MARTIN,
BENJAMIN LEVIN and BONNIE McKEE

JUST THE WAY YOU ARE

Words and Music by BRUNO MARS,
ARI LEVINE, PHILIP LAWRENCE,
KHARI CAIN and KHALIL WALTON

Moderate Hip-Hop groove

40

FIREWORK

Words and Music by MIKKEL ERIKSEN,
TOR ERIK HERMANSEN, ESTHER DEAN,
KATY PERRY and SANDY WILHELM

46

GRENADE

Words and Music by BRUNO MARS,
ARI LEVINE, PHILIP LAWRENCE,
CHRISTOPHER STEVEN BROWN, CLAUDE KELLY
and ANDREW WYATT

Eas - y come, eas - y go; that's just how you live. Oh,
take, take, take it all, but you nev - er give.
Should - 've known you was trou - ble from the first kiss; had your

HEY, SOUL SISTER

Words and Music by PAT MONAHAN,
ESPEN LIND and AMUND BJORKLAND

Moderately

Hey, _____ hey, _____ hey! _____

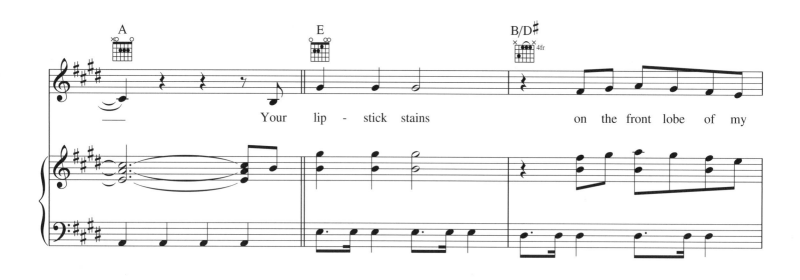

Your lip - stick stains _____ on the front lobe of my

left - side brains. I knew _ I would - n't for - get ya, and so I went and

NEED YOU NOW

Words and Music by HILLARY SCOTT,
CHARLES KELLEY, DAVE HAYWOOD
and JOSH KEAR

OMG

Words and Music by
WILL ADAMS

R&B Dance groove

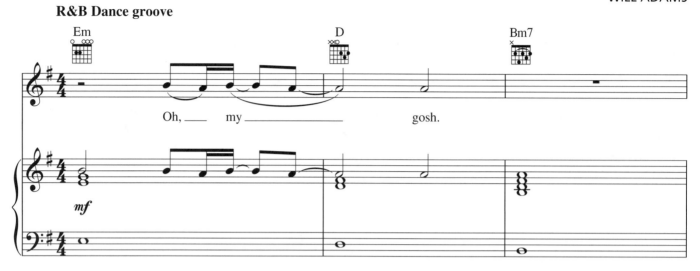

Oh, ___ my _____ gosh.

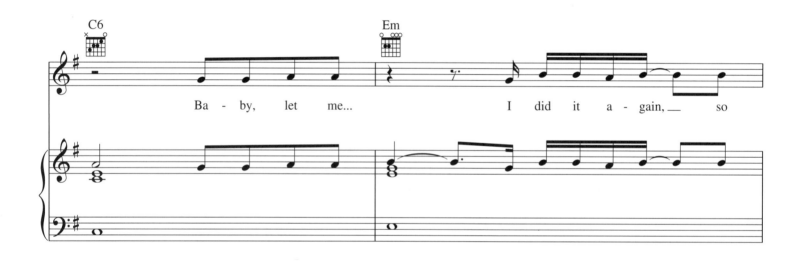

Ba - by, let me...   I did it a - gain, ___ so

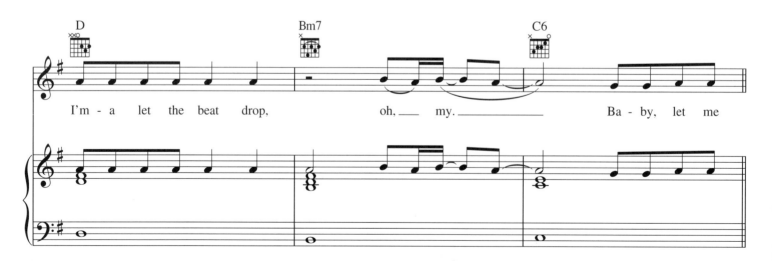

I'm - a let the beat drop,   oh, ___ my. _____   Ba - by, let me

RAISE YOUR GLASS

Words and Music by ALECIA MOORE,
MAX MARTIN and JOHAN SCHUSTER

Right, right, turn off the lights; we gon-na lose our minds to-night.
Slam, slam, oh, hot ____ damn, what part of "par - ty" don't you un - der - stand?

What's the ____ deal - i - o?
Wish you'd ____ just ____ freak out.

(2.) *(Spoken:) Freak out, already.*

TEENAGE DREAM

Words and Music by LUKASZ GOTTWALD,
MAX MARTIN, BENJAMIN LEVIN,
BONNIE McKEE and KATY PERRY

WHAT'S MY NAME?

Words and Music by MIKKEL ERIKSEN,
TOR ERIK HERMANSEN, AUBREY GRAHAM,
ESTHER DEAN and TRACY HALE

Moderate Hip-Hop groove

Oh, na, na, ___ what's my name? ___ Oh, na, na, ___ what's my name? ___

Oh, na, na, ___ what's my name? ___ Oh,

na, na, ___ what's my name? ___ Oh, na, na, ___ what's my name? ___ What's my name? ___ What's my name? ___

Additional Lyrics

Rap: Yeah, I heard you good wit' them soft lips. Yeah, you know word of mouth.
The square root of sixty nine is eight somethin', right? 'Cause I been try'n' a work it out, aaahh.
Good weed, white wine. Uh, I come alive in the nighttime. Yeah, okay, way to go.
Only thing we have on is the radio. Let it play. Say you gotta leave but I know you wanna stay.
You just waitin' on the traffic jam to finish, girl. The things that we could do with twenty minutes, girl.
Say my name. Say my name. Wear it out. It's gettin' hot, crack a window, air it out.
I could get you through a mighty long day. Soon as you go, the text that I write is gon' say...

YOUR LOVE IS MY DRUG

Words and Music by KESHA SEBERT,
JOSHUA EMANUEL COLEMAN and PEBE SEBERT

Dance Pop

Maybe I need some re-hab
Won't lis-ten to an-y ad-vice;

or may-be just need some sleep. I got a sick ob-ses-sion,
Mom's tell-ing me I should think twice. But left to my own de-vic-es,

I'm see-in' it in my dreams. I'm look-in' down ev-'ry al-ley,
I'm a-dict-ed. It's a cri-sis. My friends think I've gone cra-zy,

* Recorded a half step higher.

WE R WHO WE R

Words and Music by KESHA SEBERT, JOSHUA COLEMAN,
BENJAMIN LEVIN, LUKASZ GOTTWALD
and JACOB KASHER HINDLIN

Cm Fm E♭ A♭ Cm Fm E♭
3fr 3fr 4fr 3fr 3fr
sick and sex - i - fied, so let's go, oh, oh. Let's
A♭ Cm Fm E♭ A♭
4fr 3fr 3fr 4fr
go! To-night we're go - in' hard, hard, har, ha, ha, hard, just like the world is
Cm Fm E♭ A♭ Cm Fm E♭
3fr 3fr 4fr 3fr 3fr
our, our, our, ah, ah, ours. We're tear - in' it a - par - par - par - pa - pa -
A♭ Cm Fm E♭ A♭
4fr 3fr 3fr 4fr
part. You know we're su - per - stars; we are who we are. We're danc - in' like we're

Additional Lyrics

Rap 1: Hot and dangerous, if you're one of us then roll with us.
'Cause we make the hipsters fall in love when we've got our hot pants on enough.
And, yes, of course, we does. We runnin' this town just like a club.
And, no, you don't wanna mess with us. Got Jesus on my necklace, uss, uss.

Rap 2: Turn it up. It's about damn time to live it up.
I'm so sick of bein' so serious. It's makin' my brain delirious.
I'm just talkin' truth. I'm tellin' you 'bout the shit we do.
We're sellin' our clothes, sleepin' in cars, dressin' it down, hittin' on dudes, hard.

Big Books of Music

Our "Big Books" feature big selections of popular titles under one cover, perfect for performing musicians, music aficionados or the serious hobbyist. All books are arranged for piano, voice, and guitar, and feature stay-open binding, so the books lie flat without breaking the spine.

**BIG BOOK OF BALLADS –
2ND ED.**
62 songs.
00310485......................$19.95

BIG BOOK OF BIG BAND HITS
84 songs.
00310701......................$22.99

**BIG BOOK OF
BLUEGRASS SONGS**
70 songs.
00311484......................$19.95

BIG BOOK OF BLUES
80 songs.
00311843 ....$19.99

BIG BOOK OF BROADWAY
70 songs.
00311658......................$19.95

**BIG BOOK OF
CHILDREN'S SONGS**
55 songs.
00359261......................$14.95

**GREAT BIG BOOK OF
CHILDREN'S SONGS**
76 songs.
00310002......................$14.95

**FANTASTIC BIG BOOK OF
CHILDREN'S SONGS**
66 songs.
00311062......................$17.95

**MIGHTY BIG BOOK OF
CHILDREN'S SONGS**
65 songs.
00310467......................$14.95

**REALLY BIG BOOK OF
CHILDREN'S SONGS**
63 songs.
00310372......................$16.95

**BIG BOOK OF CHILDREN'S
MOVIE SONGS**
66 songs.
00310731......................$19.99

**BIG BOOK OF
CHRISTMAS SONGS – 2ND ED.**
126 songs.
00311520......................$19.95

BIG BOOK OF CLASSIC ROCK
77 songs.
00310801......................$22.95

**BIG BOOK OF
CLASSICAL MUSIC**
100 songs.
00310508......................$19.95

**BIG BOOK OF
CONTEMPORARY
CHRISTIAN FAVORITES –
3RD ED.**
50 songs.
00312067......................$21.99

**BIG BOOK OF COUNTRY
MUSIC – 2ND ED.**
63 songs.
00310188......................$19.95

BIG BOOK OF COUNTRY ROCK
64 songs.
00311748......................$19.99

**BIG BOOK OF EARLY
ROCK N' ROLL**
99 songs.
00310398......................$19.95

**BIG BOOK OF '50S & '60S
SWINGING SONGS**
67songs.
00310982......................$19.95

**BIG BOOK OF
FOLK POP ROCK**
79 songs.
00311125......................$24.95

BIG BOOK OF FRENCH SONGS
70 songs.
00311154......................$19.95

BIG BOOK OF GERMAN SONGS
78 songs.
00311816......................$19.99

BIG BOOK OF GOSPEL SONGS
100 songs.
00310604......................$19.95

BIG BOOK OF HYMNS
125 hymns.
00310510......................$17.95

BIG BOOK OF IRISH SONGS
76 songs.
00310981......................$19.95

**BIG BOOK OF
ITALIAN FAVORITES**
80 songs.
00311185......................$19.95

BIG BOOK OF JAZZ – 2ND ED.
75 songs.
00311557......................$19.95

**BIG BOOK OF LATIN
AMERICAN SONGS**
89 songs.
00311562......................$19.95

BIG BOOK OF LOVE SONGS
80 songs.
00310784......................$19.95

BIG BOOK OF MOTOWN
84 songs.
00311061......................$19.95

BIG BOOK OF MOVIE MUSIC
72 songs.
00311582......................$19.95

BIG BOOK OF NOSTALGIA
158 songs.
00310004......................$24.99

BIG BOOK OF OLDIES
73 songs.
00310756......................$19.95

BIG BOOK OF RAGTIME PIANO
63 songs.
00311749......................$19.95

**BIG BOOK OF
RHYTHM & BLUES**
67 songs.
00310169......................$19.95

BIG BOOK OF ROCK
78 songs.
00311566......................$22.95

BIG BOOK OF ROCK BALLADS
67 songs.
00311839......................$22.99

BIG BOOK OF SOUL
71 songs.
00310771......................$19.95

BIG BOOK OF STANDARDS
86 songs.
00311667......................$19.95

BIG BOOK OF SWING
84 songs.
00310359......................$19.95

**BIG BOOK OF
TORCH SONGS – 2ND ED.**
75 songs.
00310561......................$19.99

**BIG BOOK OF
TV THEME SONGS**
78 songs.
00310504......................$19.99

BIG BOOK OF WEDDING MUSIC
77 songs.
00311567......................$19.95

FOR MORE INFORMATION, SEE YOUR LOCAL MUSIC DEALER,
OR WRITE TO:

**HAL•LEONARD®
CORPORATION**
7777 W. BLUEMOUND RD. P.O. BOX 13819 MILWAUKEE, WI 53213

Prices, contents, and availability subject to change without notice.

Visit **www.halleonard.com**
for our entire catalog and to view our complete songlists.

0111

THE ULTIMATE SONGBOOKS

These great songbook/CD packs come with our standard arrangements for piano and voice with guitar chord frames plus a CD.
The CD includes a full performance of each song, as well as a second track without the piano part so you can play "lead" with the band!

1. MOVIE MUSIC
00311072 P/V/G $14.95

2. JAZZ BALLADS
00311073 P/V/G $14.95

3. TIMELESS POP
00311074 P/V/G $14.99

4. BROADWAY CLASSICS
00311075 P/V/G $14.95

5. DISNEY
00311076 P/V/G $14.95

6. COUNTRY STANDARDS
00311077 P/V/G $14.99

7. LOVE SONGS
00311078 P/V/G $14.95

8. CLASSICAL THEMES
00311079 PIANO SOLO $14.95

9. CHILDREN'S SONGS
0311080 P/V/G $14.95

10. WEDDING CLASSICS
00311081 Piano Solo $14.95

11. WEDDING FAVORITES
00311097 P/V/G $14.95

12. CHRISTMAS FAVORITES
00311137 P/V/G $15.95

13. YULETIDE FAVORITES
00311138 P/V/G $14.95

14. POP BALLADS
00311145 P/V/G $14.95

15. FAVORITE STANDARDS
00311146 P/V/G $14.95

17. MOVIE FAVORITES
00311148 P/V/G $14.95

18. JAZZ STANDARDS
00311149 P/V/G $14.95

19. CONTEMPORARY HITS
00311162 P/V/G $14.95

20. R&B BALLADS
00311163 P/V/G $14.95

21. BIG BAND
00311164 P/V/G $14.95

22. ROCK CLASSICS
00311165 P/V/G $14.95

23. WORSHIP CLASSICS
00311166 P/V/G $14.95

24. LES MISÉRABLES
00311169 P/V/G $14.95

25. THE SOUND OF MUSIC
00311175 P/V/G $15.99

26. ANDREW LLOYD WEBBER FAVORITES
00311178 P/V/G $14.95

27. ANDREW LLOYD WEBBER GREATS
00311179 P/V/G $14.95

28. LENNON & MCCARTNEY
00311180 P/V/G $14.95

29. THE BEACH BOYS
00311181 P/V/G $14.95

30. ELTON JOHN
00311182 P/V/G $14.95

31. CARPENTERS
00311183 P/V/G $14.95

32. BACHARACH & DAVID
00311218 P/V/G $14.95

33. PEANUTS™
00311227 P/V/G $14.95

34 CHARLIE BROWN CHRISTMAS
00311228 P/V/G $15.95

35. ELVIS PRESLEY HITS
00311230 P/V/G $14.95

36. ELVIS PRESLEY GREATS
00311231 P/V/G $14.95

37. CONTEMPORARY CHRISTIAN
00311232 P/V/G $14.95

38. DUKE ELLINGTON STANDARDS
00311233 P/V/G $14.95

39. DUKE ELLINGTON CLASSICS
00311234 P/V/G $14.95

40. SHOWTUNES
00311237 P/V/G $14.95

41. RODGERS & HAMMERSTEIN
00311238 P/V/G $14.95

42. IRVING BERLIN
00311239 P/V/G $14.95

43. JEROME KERN
00311240 P/V/G $14.95

44. FRANK SINATRA –
    POPULAR HITS
00311277 P/V/G $14.95

45. FRANK SINATRA –
    MOST REQUESTED SONGS
00311278 P/V/G $14.95

46. WICKED
00311317 P/V/G $15.99

47. RENT
00311319 P/V/G $14.95

48. CHRISTMAS CAROLS
00311332 P/V/G $14.95

49. HOLIDAY HITS
00311333 P/V/G $15.99

50. DISNEY CLASSICS
00311417 P/V/G $14.95

51. HIGH SCHOOL MUSICAL
00311421 P/V/G $19.95

52. ANDREW LLOYD WEBBER CLASSICS
00311422 P/V/G $14.95

53. GREASE
00311450 P/V/G $14.95

54. BROADWAY FAVORITES
00311451 P/V/G $14.95

FOR MORE INFORMATION,
SEE YOUR LOCAL MUSIC DEALER,
OR WRITE TO:

HAL•LEONARD®
CORPORATION
7777 W. BLUEMOUND RD. P.O. BOX 13819
MILWAUKEE, WISCONSIN 53213

Visit Hal Leonard Online at
www.halleonard.com

Prices, contents and availability
subject to change without notice.

0311

Hal Leonard
ANTHOLOGY SONGBOOKS

These collections set the gold standard for 100 prime songs at an affordable price.

All titles arranged for piano and voice with guitar chords.

ANTHOLOGY OF BROADWAY SONGS – GOLD EDITION

100 beloved songs from the Great White Way, including: All I Ask of You • Day by Day • Good Morning Baltimore • Guys and Dolls • It's De-Lovely • Makin' Whoopee! • My Favorite Things • On the Street Where You Live • Send in the Clowns • They Call the Wind Maria • Written in the Stars • Younger Than Springtime • and more.
00311954 P/V/G $24.99

ANTHOLOGY OF CHRISTMAS SONGS – GOLD EDITION

A cream-of-the-crop collection of 100 holiday favorites, both secular and sacred, including: All I Want for Christmas Is You • Carol of the Bells • Dance of the Sugar Plum Fairy • The First Noel • Jingle-Bell Rock • Joy to the World • O Christmas Tree • Santa Baby • Up on the Housetop • What Child Is This? • and more.
00311998 P/V/G $24.99

ANTHOLOGY OF COUNTRY SONGS – GOLD EDITION

100 of the best country songs ever: Always on My Mind • Butterfly Kisses • Coal Miner's Daughter • I Will Always Love You • Jackson • Mountain Music • Ring of Fire • Rocky Top • Take Me Home, Country Roads • Through the Years • Whiskey River • You Are My Sunshine • and scores more!
00312052 P/V/G $24.99

ANTHOLOGY OF JAZZ SONGS – GOLD EDITION

This solid collection of jazz favorites boasts 100 songs that set the gold standard for jazz classics! Includes: All of You • April in Paris • Come Fly with Me • From This Moment On • I Got It Bad and That Ain't Good • In the Mood • Lazy River • St. Louis Blues • Stormy Weather (Keeps Rainin' All the Time) • When I Fall in Love • and dozens more.
00311952 P/V/G $24.99

ANTHOLOGY OF LATIN SONGS – GOLD EDITION

100 Latin-flavored favorites, including: Bésame Mucho (Kiss Me Much) • Cast Your Fate to the Wind • Desafinado • La Bamba • Mas Que Nada • One Note Samba (Samba De Uma Nota So) • Quiet Nights of Quiet Stars (Corcovado) • So Nice (Summer Samba) • Spanish Eyes • Sway (Quien Sera) • and more.
00311956 P/V/G $24.99

ANTHOLOGY OF LOVE SONGS – GOLD EDITION

This fantastic collection features 100 songs full of love and romance, including: And I Love You So • Cheek to Cheek • Crazy • Fields of Gold • Grow Old with Me • Just the Way You Are • Love Me Tender • On a Slow Boat to China • Take My Breath Away (Love Theme) • A Time for Us (Love Theme) • Unchained Melody • When I Need You • and more.
00311955 P/V/G $24.99

ANTHOLOGY OF MOVIE SONGS – GOLD EDITION

An outstanding collection of favorite cinema songs, including: Bella's Lullaby • Dancing Queen • Georgia on My Mind • I Will Always Love You • Love Story • Mission: Impossible Theme • Theme from The Simpsons • Take My Breath Away (Love Theme) • A Whole New World • You Are the Music in Me • and many more.
00311967 P/V/G $24.99

ANTHOLOGY OF R&B SONGS – GOLD EDITION

100 R&B classics are included in this collection: ABC • Brick House • Get Ready • I Say a Little Prayer • It's Your Thing • Mustang Sally • Please Mr. Postman • Respect • This Old Heart of Mine (Is Weak for You) • What'd I Say • and more.
00312016 P/V/G $24.99

ANTHOLOGY OF ROCK SONGS – GOLD EDITION

This amazing collection features 100 rock hits, including: Africa • Bad, Bad Leroy Brown • Chantilly Lace • December 1963 (Oh, What a Night) • Fun, Fun, Fun • A Hard Day's Night • Layla • Night Moves • Ramblin' Man • That'll Be the Day • We Will Rock You • and many more.
00311953 P/V/G $24.99

FOR MORE INFORMATION, SEE YOUR LOCAL MUSIC DEALER, OR WRITE TO:

HAL•LEONARD® CORPORATION

7777 W. BLUEMOUND RD. P.O. BOX 13819 MILWAUKEE, WI 53213

Visit Hal Leonard Online at
www.halleonard.com

Prices, contents, and availability subject to change without notice.

0111